13 STEPS TO EVIL

HOW TO CRAFT A SUPERBAD VILLAIN WORKBOOK

SACHA BLACK

13 STEPS TO EVIL – HOW TO CRAFT SUPERBAD VILLAINS – THE WORKBOOK

By Sacha Black

READ ME FIRST

If you've read the full companion book, *13 Steps To Evil: How To Craft A Superbad Villain*, you'll know that I'm biased. While I think heroes are interesting, I also believe they're predictable. World saving on repeat can get a little dull. Readers want tension, grit, emotion, and conflict. Besides, it's much more satisfying to craft a character with an evil glint in their eye than a stoic halo polishing god. Do you want to create a bad guy who's so unpredictable even you don't know what they'll do next? Or would you rather have a copycat warlord with no motives and a questionable disposition towards clichés and the color black?

I think we both know the answer because you wouldn't be reading this if you didn't. But, while knowing you want to get your bad boy right, and reading a book telling you how might be handy, without putting it into practice, you're going to reside firmly in the apprentice camp and Yoda is going to leave you for space dust.

Malcom Gladwell is famed for arguing that it takes 10,000 hours of deliberate practice in order to become an expert at something. While I'm not suggesting you need to practice creating villains for 10,000 hours before you create a decent one, I am saying that you need to put the lessons into practice. This is a workbook. There are exercises. Do them. Do them again. Then put what you learn into your manuscripts.

Some points to note:

During explanations in this book, I predominantly use the term villain. Villains and antagonists *are* different, and I explain why in a moment. But, for the sake of simplicity, I'll stick to villain. Just apply whichever term is most relevant to your story.

This is a workbook. It deliberately assumes that you've either read the full book or that you already understand many of the story building concepts in here, which gives you the time and space to complete the exercises to help you craft the best villain you can.

If you want the detail behind the book, then you'll need to read 13 Steps To Evil cover to cover. But I've tried to add enough information to each step so that you should be able to understand the concepts.

If you want to sell the books you bleed, then you'll also need to know your market and that, young pad wan, **is why many of the questions in here are focused on your genre or market.** You need to be at one with your genre; merge with it like a big white fluffy polar bear camouflaged in the Arctic. Readers read genres for a reason; it's like going home for them. They know what's behind the first-page-front-door and there are certain things villains from their hometown will, and won't do. You need to know these things because there's a cocktail of nuances and tropes in each genre. Some you can bat away like dead flies; others your readers will expect you to adhere to and if you don't, the villain police will come and arrest you. Okay, that's a lie. There are no villain police, but your readers will expect you to adhere to some tropes.

During the book all questions will be labelled with a 'Q.' All spaces for answers will be labelled 'A' where only one answer is required and with a number, i.e. 'A.1, A.2,' depending on how many answers that particular question requires.

Before we start, let's make sure you're going to get what you need. **There are four reasons you should stop reading now:**

One: If you're here to learn about writing horror, then stop now; thank you for picking this book up, but it's not for you. I am not a horror writer, and although many aspects of villainy are translatable to horror, this book is devoted to villains more broadly and particularly to developing their character.

Two: You write literary fiction or fiction that doesn't easily sit in a genre. Most of the examples in this book come from genre fiction. While you may be able to take elements of the lessons from this book into general fiction, I don't cover it specifically.

Three: If you're sensitive in any way, don't like bad words, odd explanations, or dodgy humor, you might wanna leave before things get ugly.

Four: You don't like doing creative writing exercises.

Still with me? Then welcome on board.

Let's get our villain on.

STEP 1 THE BASICS OF VILLAINY

Why Writers Fudge Up Their Villains

Before we develop a villain, we need to understand why so many writers get them wrong.

Villains are like newborn infants. So much glorious potential. Until we writers get our grubby mitts on them and balls it up. With the careless flick of a pen, we can turn a finely sculpted baby villain into a cringe-worthy cliché because we don't make him bad enough, or we create something so heinously evil it's unrealistic.

While researching for the book, writers told me all kinds of problems they encountered while creating their villains. From getting the dialogue right and avoiding clichés, to knowing how evil to make a villain, to how to reveal her motives without using blatant exposition.

But behind all these issues are two basic barriers that are the Achilles in every writer's villainous heel:

1. Depending on the point of view (POV) the book's written in, the villain is *usually* seen through the eyes of your hero.

A solitary POV gives you a page-limited amount of time to show your villain's best, most authentic, and devilishly evil side. Page-limited to the point it makes it eye-wateringly difficult to convey her backstory effectively without information dumping. You have to be better, clearer, more tactical, and more concise with your words to create superbad villains.

2. Writers are hero worshippers.

We love our heroes and protagonists more than our spouses. And as a result, we spend shameful amounts of time honing our protagonist's muscular heroics into shape. But that relegates our villain (the plot-driving conflict-creator) to the corner of our book, complete with a nobody-loves-you-anyway hat. In other words, writers don't pay enough attention to their villain.

When a new born arrives onto this planet most parents are concerned with what gender the tiny homunculus is. While gender is less pressing for a villain, establishing what *kind* of bad guy they are is important. Because 'villain' doesn't always mean raging warlord with a beard, a 10,000-strong army and a penchant for wands. In fact, villain, doesn't always mean villain. Sometimes it's an antagonist. To confuse things more, sometimes the hero isn't the protagonist either.

Let's unravel this with an example. In *The Silence of the Lambs*, Hannibal Lecter is a villain, but he is also the protagonist. That's because the story is about him, and what he did. But the hero of the story is Clarice Starling, an FBI agent trying to solve the crimes of another serial killer. In *Gone Girl,* there are two protagonists: a couple, one of whom turns out to be the villain.

- The difference between a villain and an antagonist is that a villain is evil, an antagonist isn't, but they **both** oppose the hero.
- The difference between a hero and a protagonist is that a hero has a superhuman ability for good, whereas the protagonist is who the story is about.

Plotter or pantser, eventually, every writer needs to know the basics of their villain. Some writers interview their characters, others write diary entries, others still let their characters form on the page. There are no wrong answers with character creation. But for the sake of a consistent story, you do need to keep a note, however short, of the distinguishing features your villain has.

QUICK TIP - Create A Book-Bible. A book bible is a document or list that notes down all the key information an editor (or a writer editing their book) would need.

Things to include in your book bible:

- Character names
- Character descriptions
- The spelling of unusual words
- Any capitalisation of unusual words
- Description of key locations and the weather or distinguishing features
- Any society laws or rules that can't be broken
- A story timeline
- Character motivations

You don't need to include any or all of these suggestions; make your book bible your own. But having one is handy for editors to know what to look for in terms of spellings and capitalisations.

EXERCISE: Go create your book-bible!

In 13 Steps To Evil, I explain that the most important part of your novel isn't plot or characters as a lot of writers think, but conflict. And where does conflict come from? Your villain. Think about it. Without Lex Luthor would we even need Superman...? Exactly. And that's the point. Your book needs conflict like you need oxygen.

For more information on the basics of villainy, check out Step 1 in 13 Steps To Evil (pages 11 to 20).

DEVELOPING MARKET KNOWLEDGE EXERCISES

Q. Think of three of your favorite books. Can you identify the central conflict in each one?

A.1.

.

.

A.2.

.

.

A.3.

.

.

Q. Do the same for your favorite three books in the genre you write (if it's different to the books you just thought of).

A.1.

.

.

A.2.

.

.

A.3.

.

.

I mentioned *Gone Girl* and *The Silence of the Lambs* as two exam-ples where the protagonist was not the hero.

Q. Can you think of any more examples from any genre, and what about the genre you write in?

Any genre

A.1.

.

.

A.2.

.

.

Your genre

A.1.

.

.

A.2.

.

.

Q. From all of the examples above, note down any patterns you see, or points that you like about the stories, or villains.

A.

.

.

.

.

DEVELOPING YOUR VILLAIN EXERCISES

Q. What type of villain should you have? Villain, antagonist, or anti-hero?

A.

   Q. What type of hero should you have? Hero, protagonist, or anti-hero?

A.

   Q. What is your core conflict?

A.
.

.

.

   Q. Core conflict description:

A.
.

.

.

Q. If you have additional conflicts, or subplots that generate conflict, note those down too. For example, a family dispute or perhaps a love triangle.

Additional Conflict 1

.

.

.

Additional Conflict 2

.

.

.

Q. Name three barriers (conflict) your villain puts in your hero's way.

A.1.

.

.

A.2.

.

.

A.3.

.

.

Q. Describe why these barriers benefit your villain.

A.1.

.

.

A.2.

.

.

A.3.

.

.

Q. What does your villain have to sacrifice to beat your hero?

A.

.

.

.

Q. How does the story affect the villain? Do they get more evil and bitter? Is this as a result of their traits or their choices?

A.

.

.

.

For the plotters out there, in the appendices, you'll find a non-exhaustive list of questions you can ask yourself about your villain so you can get a basic handle on them. I've put it at the back, rather than in here because some of the questions will be easier to answer after reading this book.

STEP 2 TRAITS

Humans are messy and confusing but more often than not, we react predictably to events because we are creatures of habit. Which means we're consistent until suddenly, we're not. But our spontaneity is what makes us unique. Nonetheless, to have a different reaction to something, you first have to establish 'character' and normal behaviors. That's where traits come in.

Traits are the facets of personality that produce consistent behavior. The trick with traits is to recognise that you write fiction, not realism. Readers aren't expecting real humans to climb out of the pages because they know books aren't real. They need just enough depth for characters to be a reflection of reality.

The point is, you don't have enough pages to accurately portray your villain as a multifaceted human. So don't try. A small handful of traits used consistently will pack the power of a literary atom bomb.

QUICK TIP – Trait Picking.
Tip 1: You can't have a villain without at least one negative trait.
Tip 2: You need to include at least one positive trait.
Tip 3: Pick whatever traits you want, but bear trait polarity in mind.

What's trait polarity? Well, most heroes and villains have opposing core traits. But you don't have to create your villain as the opposite of your hero. There are lots of examples where hero and villain have the same or similar traits. Think Thor and Loki from *Thor* (from the *Marvel* Universe). They're brothers who share similar arrogant traits.

Readers love the hero because he embodies your book's theme: he is what the book is about. Which is why the villain must represent the anti-theme.

Character Example: Katniss in The Hunger Games by Suzanne Collins – Katniss embodies the book's theme: self-sacrifice by taking the place of her sister in the Reaping (an event likely to kill her sister). But President Snow (the villain) is the exact opposite. The only thing he ever sacrifices is other people.

QUICK TIP – Foreshadow Downfall. If your villain starts out as 'good' or with your readers sympathizing with them, then you need to foreshadow their downfall. Otherwise your readers will feel cheated.

For more information on traits, check out Step 2 in 13 Steps To Evil (pages 21 to 35).

DEVELOPING MARKET KNOWLEDGE EXERCISES

Think about your three favorite villains from any movie, book or TV series in the genre you write in.

Q. Name their positive and negative traits. Are there any patterns to the traits?

Villain 1
Positive
A.1.

.

.

.

A.2.

.

.

.

A.3.

.

.

.

Negative

A.1.

.

.

.

A.2.

.

.

.

A.3.

.

.

.

Villain 2
Positive
A.1.

.

.

.

A.2.

.

.

.

A.3.

.

.

.

Negative
A.1.

.

.

.

A.2.

.

.

.

A.3.

.

.

.

Villain 3

Positive

A.1.

.

.

.

A.2.

.

.

.

A.3.

.

.

.

Negative

A.1.

.

.

.

A.2.

.

.

.

A.3.

.

.

.

Q. Are there any patterns or similarities to the traits? And what is the balance between positive and negative?

A.

.

.

.

.

DEVELOPING YOUR VILLAIN EXERCISES

Q. Think about your friends, family, colleagues at work, cousin's sister's friend's dog walker. Anyone and everyone you know. Note down three odd quirks or traits they have that would suit a character in a book.

A.1.

.

.

.

A.2.

.

.

.

A.3.

.

.

.

Q. What positive and negative traits have you given your villain?

Positive

A.1.

.

.

.

A.2.

.

.

.

A.3.

.

.

.

Negative
A.1.

.

.

.

A.2.

.

.

.

A.3.

.

.

.

Q. Now name your hero's positive and negative traits.

Positive
A.1.

.

.

.

A.2.

.

.

·

A.3.

·

·

·

Q. Who or what does your hero love that your villain could use to defeat the hero?

A.

·

·

·

·

Q. Will your readers sympathize with your villain early on? If yes, how and where have you foreshadowed their evil inner core?

A.

·

·

·

·

Q. Compare your villain's traits to your hero's. How will the traits interact? Are there similarities or differences that can increase the conflict between them?

Similarities

-

-

-

-

Differences

-

-

-

-

How can these interact to increase conflict?

-

-

-

-

There's a list of traits in the appendices to help you narrow down your villain's personality and to help you define the traits of your genre's villains.

STEP 3 MOTIVES AND GOALS

The word 'why' is the source of everything human. It gives us our purpose, drives our motivations and goals. **If your villain has no real motive, neither does your hero. Likewise, if your hero has no real motive, then neither does your villain.** It's chicken and egg. Actually, screw the chicken *and* the egg. Motives are more fundamental than even the primordial sludge, and without that prehistoric mud pie, we wouldn't be here, so motives are pretty freaking important.

Why is it so important? Because a motive is justification for behavior, and that gives your villain depth. It also gives your hero a reason and motive to fight back.

Motives are also inextricably linked to conflict.

No motive, no conflict. No conflict, no story.

The goal is the *what* a villain wants, the real sticky hold-in-your-hands 'thing' a villain wants to do, or achieve, or destroy. The motive is the reason *why* he wants it. And to be a fully rounded villain, he needs both a motive and a goal.

Most heroes and villains will have opposing goals, but they don't have to.

Without proper motives and goals your villain is going to be one of three things:

1. A cliché
2. Have no depth
3. Be unbelievable

If you'd like more information on creating motives and goals then check step 3 pages 36 to 47 in 13 Steps To Evil.

DEVELOPING MARKET KNOWLEDGE EXERCISES

Think about your three favorite villains from your genre. Answer the following:

Q. What is their goal?

Villain 1

.

.

.

Villain 2

.

.

.

Villain 3

.

.

.

.

Q. What are their motives?

Villain 1

.

.

.

Villain 2

.

.

.

Villain 3

.

.

.

Q. What barrier/s does each villain put in their hero's way?

Villain 1

.

.

.

Villain 2

.

.

.

Villain 3

.

.

.

Q. Are there any patterns/tropes to the motives, goals, and barriers a villain in your genre puts in the hero's way?

A.

.

.

.

DEVELOPING YOUR VILLAIN EXERCISES

Q. List as many motives or reasons 'why' a villain would want to defeat a hero as you can.

A.

.

.

.

Q. What is your villain striving for in your story (what's her goal)?

A.

.

.

.

Q. Why is this goal so important to her (what's her motive)?

A.

.

.

.

Q. Where does her motive come from? Is there a history behind it or any particular events that led her to her motive?

A.

.

.

.

Q. How and when in your plot does whatever she's striving for, become a barrier to your hero achieving his goal?

A.

.

.

.

Q. What other obstacles will she put in the hero's way?

A.

-

-

-

-

-

-

-

Q. What's your villain's plan to reach her goal – i.e. how does your villain plan to defeat your hero?

A.

-

-

-

-

-

-

-

-

Q. Will she need to double cross the hero to reach her goal? If yes, how?

A.

.

.

.

.

.

.

Q. What's your hero's goal and motive?

A.

.

.

.

.

Q. Look back at all your notes, and summarise in one sentence your villain's 'why.'

A.

.

.

.

STEP 4 THE HISTORY OF VILLAIN PSYCHOLOGY

Understanding the cause of a character's behavior enables you to give them and their reactions to your plot more depth. The source, more often than not, is our history. It shapes and influences how we see the world and subsequently how we react to it.

The parts of our history that shape us the most in life are those that are the most emotional. For example, not reaching a parent's death bed, losing a limb, going through a divorce, or saving someone's life. I call these experiences, soul scars.

Soul scars are the experiences that leave a mark (positive or negative) on our lives, to the extent that some part of us changes after the experience. Soul scars influence our behaviors, thoughts, decision making, and actions. That's why they are a great source for developing a villain's motive.

QUICK TIP - Everything comes down to choice. Although experiences and soul scars shape a person, it's how a person reacts to them that defines who they are and what they become. What separates a villain from a hero are the choices and decisions they make.

Repeated experiences linked to a soul scar (especially when negative) can lead your villain to develop a psychological complex.

A complex is a pattern of experiences (emotional, physical, etc.) that form in a person's unconscious mind and influence future behaviors, attitudes, and thoughts. It is also a protective mechanism that works unconsciously to counteract the negative emotions a person has formed about themselves. Its purpose is to move a person from a negative mind set to a positive one. This is why it influences decision making and leads a villain to make bad choices.

QUICK TIP – Character Arcs. One way to create a character arc is to create a false truth about the character that they believe: i.e. a lie. For example, Thor from the *Marvel* movie believed he was unworthy of power. This lie is proven false right before the climax of the film when he discovers the truth about himself: he is worthy, he just has to be a selfless leader.

But with a villain, the opposite is true. Loki, Thor's brother, also believes he is unworthy, however, instead of having that lie proved false, it's proven true.

This creates a situation where the villain has nothing to lose and they believe there's no salvation because of the lie. A person with nothing to lose is dangerous, even more so when they have the mindset of a villain.

The easiest and simplest way to differentiate between your hero and your villain's arc is as reversals of each other.

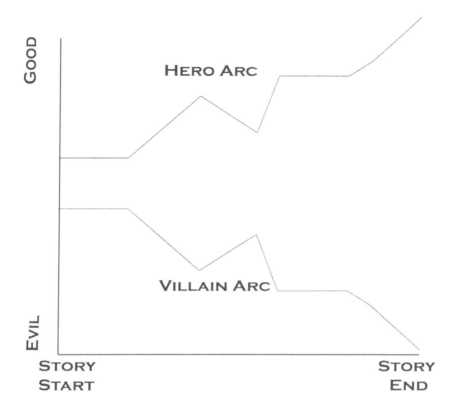

There's a neat way to summarize everything I've just said:

SOUL SCARS + NEGATIVE TRAITS = COMPLEXES which = THE LIE YOUR VILLAIN BELIEVES which leads to BAD DECISIONS.

If you'd like more information on creating the perfect history then check step 4 pages 48 to 66 in 13 Steps To Evil.

DEVELOPING MARKET KNOWLEDGE EXERCISES

Q. Think about three villains in your genre from film, TV or books. What lie or lies do they believe?

Villain 1

-

-

-

-

Villain 2

-

-

-

-

Villain 3

-

-

-

-

Q. What lie or lies do the heroes in the same stories believe?

Hero 1

-

-

-

Hero 2

-

·

·

Hero 3

Q. Name three villains and their associated soul scars from your genre.

Villain 1

·

·

·

·

Villain 2

·

·

·

·

Villain 3

·

·

·

·

Q. Can you think of any fictional villains from your genre that have a complex?

Villain 1

.

.

.

.

Villain 2

.

.

.

.

Villain 3

.

.

.

.

Take one of those villains and deconstruct their character:
Q. What events or experiences led them to form the complex?

A.

.

.

.

.

.

.

.

Q. What event was the final straw in the villain's history that pushed them over into a complex and villainy?

A.

.

.

.

.

.

.

Q. What soul scar does that villain have?

A.

.

.

.

·

·

Q. What techniques could you replicate from the way the author structured the villain's history to use in your own story structure?

A.

·

·

·

·

·

·

DEVELOPING YOUR VILLAIN EXERCISES

Q. Have a look at the list of soul scars in the back. Can you add five more soul scars to the list?

A.1.

A.2.

A.3.

A.4.

A.5.

Q. What is or are your villain's personal soul scars?

A.1.

A.2.

A.3.

Q. What defining experience or experiences led your villain to his soul scar?

A.

.

.

.

.

Q. What bad decisions does your villain's complex lead him to make?

A.

.

.

.

.

.

Q. What lie does your villain believe?

A.

.

.

.

.

.

Q. If you're not using a lie to facilitate the character arc, what actions or plot points prompt your villain's descent into villainy?

A.

.

.

.

.

.

.

Q. Does your hero have any soul scars?

A.1.

.

.

A.2.

.

.

A.3.

.

.

Q. What lie or lies does your hero believe? And how is this lie disproved?

A.

.

.

.

.

.

Q. What does your villain want that your hero will end up with? What's the impact of that on your villain's mindset and future actions?

A.

.

.

.

-

-

-

Q. What action does your hero take or what moment in the plot solidifies your villain as the bad guy?

A.
-

-

-

-

-

Q. How does your villain react in that moment and how is that reaction linked to their past and their soul scar?

A.
-

-

-

-

-

Q. What situation in your plot makes your villain believe the lie is true?

A.

.

.

.

STEP 5 CREDIBILITY AND AUTHENTICITY

Credibility is about being believable and creating trust in the reader. In other words, you need to make them trust that your villain really will chop off Aunt Gertie's fingers if her reprobate nephew doesn't pay up.

Credibility + Believability = An Authentic Villain

QUICK TIP – Value A Villain's Values. One fast way to gain believability is to give your villain some inner values. By value, I mean something that has some kind of worth or importance. There are two ways values can be incorporated into a villain's character.

1. Giving your villain a positive value that they display in a bad way, i.e. your villain values loyalty and severely punishes anyone who is un-loyal.

2. Giving your villain a negative value, that they display in a bad way, i.e. valuing murder as a useful tool to get ahead.

Character Example: Lord Voldemort from the Harry Potter series by J.K.

Rowling – Lord Voldemort is a classic example of a villain who places a high value on loyalty. So much so, he brands his followers with the Dark Mark and kills anyone who changes their mind and wants out.

The point is, everyone has values. But what defines whether they're a hero or villain, is how a character reacts when those values are broken.

Another way to build believability fast is to use the traits you've given your villain to create consistent behaviors. People are unfailingly reliable: we have habits and ticks. Your villain will too. You also don't need a hundred different traits to make a character or a villain real; you just need to show a small handful consistently.

Credibility is often born from having integrity. And a villain, despite all their faults, can have integrity if they stick to their moral, ethical or value based principles. Even if those morals are warped. Think of a villain as a leader. Authentic leaders do exactly what they say they will, even when that's hard or painful.

Your villain also needs to be hard to beat because the fight between hero and villain needs to be just that: a fight. In real life, your villain has to be strong enough to give your hero a run for his money, not just physically but mentally too or your plot won't carry enough tension related ups and downs.

QUICK TIP – Knowing The Inevitable. You can add a level of credibility to your villain by ensuring the hero knows your villain is coming for him and why, but don't let the reader know how or when, to keep the story's mystery and your reader on the edge of their seat.

If you'd like more information on creating credibility then check step 5 pages 67 to 79 in 13 Steps To Evil.

DEVELOPING MARKET KNOWLEDGE EXERCISES

Q. Write a list of at least five villains you think are credible, authentic, and believable. Try to have at least three of them from your genre.

A.1.

.

A.2.

.

A.3.

.

A.4.

.

A.5.

.

Q. Write another list of five villains you don't think are credible or believable, and try to have three that are from your genre.

A.1.

.

A.2.

.

A.3.

.

A.4.

.

A.5.

.

Q. Of the three credible villains in your genre, name their top one or two values.

Villain 1
Value 1

.

.

Value 2

.

.

Q. Are their values positive, negative, or a mixture, and if they're a mixture, what is the balance between good and bad?

Value 1

.

.

Value 2

.

.

Q. How does this villain react when one of their values is broken?

Villain 2
Value 1

·

·

Value 2

·

·

Q. Are their values positive, negative, or a mixture, and if they're a mixture, what is the balance between good and bad?

Value 1

·

·

Value 2

·

·

Q. How does this villain react when one of their values is broken?

Villain 3
Value 1

·

·

Value 2

·

·

Q. Are their values positive, negative, or a mixture, and if they're a mixture, what is the balance between good and bad?

Value 1

·

·

Value 2

·

·

Q. How does this villain react when one of their values is broken?

A.

·

·

·

·

DEVELOPING YOUR VILLAIN EXERCISES

Q. Use the list at the back of the book to choose some values for your villain. List their values and morals:

A.

·

-

-

-

-

Q. Does your villain have negative values, or positive values enacted in a negative way?

A.

-

-

-

-

-

Q. How does this further the plot and tension?

A.

-

-

-

-

Q. How will your villain react when their values are broken?

A.

．

．

．

Q. What is your villain an expert in? Or what will they be better than the hero at which will make the fight difficult for the hero?

A.

．

．

．

．

Q. How does your villain show integrity? I. e. how do they stick to their values no matter what? Even if the results are bad ones.

A.

．

．

．

．

STEP 6 50 SHADES OF VILLAIN

Villains don't always have to be people, nor do they have to be pure evil, and they don't even have to be a person at all. But, like people, there is always a pattern to their behavior. With villains, it's easier to categorise them. Some like to think of these categories as archetypes.

Villain Archetypes

Omnipotent Power Hungry Dark Lord – This is an old-school power hungry, slightly crazy-eyed, occasionally demonic, but ultimately a seriously powerful villain like Sauron from *Lord of the Rings*, or Lord Voldemort from *Harry Potter*.

The Arch Nemesis – This villain doesn't start out evil, but with the hero's growing success, his jealousy and bitterness grows. Think Draco Malfoy from *Harry Potter*.

The Deranged Lunatic - Most commonly, psychopaths or sociopaths don't tend to have solid motivations for their crimes. Think Hannibal Lecter from *The Silence of The Lambs*.

The Revenge Whore - She uses her revenge and whatever happened to her in the past as justification for committing crimes. While the revenge villain might seem similar to an arch nemesis, the difference is, this villain doesn't have to have a vendetta against the hero specifically, or at least not to start with. Think Freddie Krueger from *A Nightmare on Elm Street* or Two-Face from *The Dark Knight*.

The Secret Squirrel - This villain is all about betrayal, secrets, lies, and super mega awesome plot twists. You know when you have to put a book down because a killer twist was revealed and you need a moment to pick your jaw off the floor and replace it back with your teeth? Well, this villain does that. Think Annie Wilkes from *Misery* or Amy from *Gone Girl*.

QUICK TIP – Misdirect Don't Cheat. Caution: this villain involves misdirecting the reader. That's fine, but you need to sow a seed of doubt, however small, in your reader's mind, so they don't feel cheated.

The Invisible Internal Villain – In some ways, this is the ultimate villain because he is so super bad he *really is* nearly unbeatable. The protagonist has to make enormous sacrifices and go through huge developmental arcs to be able to defeat the hardest villain of them all, himself. Think Tyler Durden from *Fight Club* or Venom from *Spiderman*.

The Slut Seductress - The female slut villain is a cliché. And is usually a tall, leggy, gorgeous, blond (or brunette for that matter), high heel wearing sexual predator. Think Debbie Jellinsky from *Addams Family Values*, and Catherine Tramell from *Basic Instinct*.

The Jealous One - The jealous one is usually, although not always, a sibling or family relation. You can often find examples in high school stories and films. But anywhere where there are two related characters. Think the ugly stepsisters in *Cinderella* or Loki - Thor's adopted brother from *Thor*.

QUICK TIP – Female Villains. People think there's a magic trick needed for female villains. But it's a distraction. Villainy isn't determined by a pair of boobs, it's determined by a villain's actions. You don't have to do anything different when crafting a female villain than when crafting a male one. Focus on the same aspects: *credibility, core values, integrity, authenticity, expertise, and believability.*

If you'd like more information on archetypes then check step 6 pages 80 to 98 in 13 Steps To Evil.

DEVELOPING MARKET KNOWLEDGE EXERCISES

Q. Name one villain from each archetype.

Omnipotent Dark Lord -

Arch Nemesis -

Deranged Lunatic -

Revenge Whore -

Secret Squirrel -

Internal Villain -

Slut Seductress -

Jealous One -

Q. Try to do the same only stick to your genre. Is there one villain of each archetype?

Omnipotent Dark Lord -

Arch Nemesis -

Deranged Lunatic -

Revenge Whore -

Secret Squirrel -

Internal Villain -

Slut Seductress -

Jealous One -

Q. Think of five villains from your genre and five from other genres. What archetype of villain do they fit into?
Your genre: (name and archetype)

A.1.

.

A.2.

.

A.3.

.

A.4.

.

A.5.

.

Other genres: (name and archetype)

A.1.

.

A.2.

.

A.3.

.

A.4.

.

A.5.

.

Q. Can you spot similarities in the way those villains are constructed? Are there certain elements or tropes you like that you can see across the archetypes?

A.

.

.

.

Q. Is there a certain type of villain found more frequently in your genre?

A.

.

.

.

Q. Think of five female villains. What archetype do they fit into?

A.1.

.

A.2.

.

A.3.

.

A.4.

.

A.5.

.

Q. Do these female villains show any patterns or similarities in their arcs, motives, or traits?

A.

•

•

•

•

DEVELOPING YOUR VILLAIN EXERCISES

Q. Which archetype does your villain fall into?

A.

•

•

•

Q. What is it about your villain that classifies them as that particular archetype?

A.

•

•

•

Q. Does your **hero** have an internal demon to face as well as your villain? If yes, how can your villain use your hero's inner demon to his advantage?

A.

.

.

.

Q. What archetype patterns or tropes do you need to adhere to within your genre?

A.

.

.

.

.

Q. Are there any aspects of the other archetypes that you could write into your own villain to increase the tension and conflict?

A.

.

.

.

.

STEP 7 ANTI-HEROES

Anti-heroes are a perfectly balanced hybrid of hero and villain. They're flawed heroes that not only have negative personality traits but engage in bad behaviors too and those behaviors are typically seen as uncharacteristic of a hero. But it's their redeeming qualities that lead them to make the right decision at the end of the story, and that's what keeps them a hero.

But that doesn't mean an anti-hero's motives for saving the day are always good and as pure as a knight in shining armor.

QUICK TIP – **Anti-heroes Have Standards**! – They usually have a moral or ethical line they won't cross. Like Robin Hood, who is a thief but justifies his behavior by only robbing rich people.

Anti-heroes make two types of decisions:

1. Bad decisions for the right reasons or
2. Good decisions for the wrong reasons

For example, Robin hood makes a bad decision (to rob people) but for the right reason – so he can give the money to poor people who need it.

QUICK TIP – Anti-heroes' Arc – unlike heroes who go through significant character development as your story progresses, anti-heroes rarely change. They just make better decisions. For example, Deadpool (from the *Marvel* universe) stops being arrogant, sucks up his ego and asks for help, which results in him saving the love of his life.

However, even though an anti-hero redeems himself with some delightful act of heroism during your story's climax, if you have to remove the 'anti' i.e. the negative traits, so he makes the right choice, then he isn't an anti-hero at all. He's a flawed hero.

Just like villains, anti-heroes have weaknesses. Using their weakness is the easiest way to get them to convert to making the right decision for the right reason. That's because their weakness usually comes from their core, and is often (although not always) derived from their love of someone or something other than themselves. When it isn't linked to something they love, it's linked to their flaw.

Because an anti-hero isn't your typical hero, you don't have to stick to accepted notions of what a hero is. Why not mess with an anti-hero's appearance too, like Deadpool's scarred face.

QUICK TIP – Where Does The Bad Come From? The source of your anti-hero's bad behavior doesn't have to be his traits. It can also be reflected in his means of seeking justice i.e. his 'means.'

If you'd like more information on anti-heroes then check step 7 pages 99 to 115 in 13 Steps To Evil.

DEVELOPING MARKET KNOWLEDGE EXERCISES

Q. List three examples of anti-heroes from outside your genre.

A.1.

.

A.2.

.

A.3.

.

Q. Now list five examples of anti-heroes from your genre.

A.1.

.

A.2.

.

A.3.

.

A.4.

.

A.5.

.

Q. Of the anti-heroes in your genre, what types of decisions do they make?

Anti-hero 1

-

-

Anti-hero 2

-

-

Anti-hero 3

-

-

Anti-hero 4

-

-

Anti-hero 5

-

-

Q. Are there any patterns to the types of decisions anti-heroes make in your genre?

A.

-

-

-

DEVELOPING YOUR VILLAIN EXERCISES

Q. What bad traits does your anti-hero have?

A.

•

•

•

Q. What bad behavior does your anti-hero regularly engage in?

A.

•

•

•

Q. What means does your anti-hero use to get what he wants? I.e. is he violent or verbally clever?

A.

•

•

•

Q. How might his bad behavior create tension between him and the villain or the hero in the plot?

A.

•

.

.

Q. What are the consequences of your anti-hero's bad behavior? I.e. How can your anti-hero's bad behavior cause problems for him in achieving his goals in the plot?

A.

.

.

.

Q. What type of decisions does your anti-hero make?

A.

.

.

.

Q. List your anti-hero's decisions during your plot and the justifications for them e.g. three bad decisions and the 'right reasons' or three good decisions for the 'wrong reasons.'

Decision 1

.

.

.

Reason 1

.

.

.

Decision 2

.

.

.

Reason 2

.

.

.

Decision 3

.

.

.

Reason 3

.

.

.

Q. What action or situation in the plot forces your anti-hero to make the right decision for the right reason and save the day?

A.

·

·

·

·

Q. At what point in your plot is this decision made? Is it close enough to the climax of your story?

A.

·

·

·

·

Q. What action does your anti-hero take to save the day and redeem himself?

A.

·

·

·

·

Q. What lesson does your anti-hero learn as a result of the action that leads him to make better decision making?

A.

.

.

.

.

Q. What good traits does your anti-hero have?

A.

.

.

.

.

Q. What's the one thing your anti-hero cares about more than himself? I.e. what thing or person will push your anti-hero to make the right decision for the right reason?

A.

.

.

.

.

Q. Does your anti-hero have any unusual physical features? If yes, describe them.

A.

.

.

.

.

STEP 8 CLICHÉS

Everyone can spot a cliché because it induces wincing, grimaces and surreptitious glances. But, as a writer, you don't want one sneaking into your manuscript.

Classic cliché examples include:

- 'Objection' used in a court scene when the prosecutor is losing
- A villain or a witch with a 'muhahaha' laugh or a cackle
- They all lived happily ever after
- The priest saying 'Does anyone object?' and the protagonist's true love bursting into the church
- And then I woke up and realized it was all a dream

Did they make you cringe? Cause I felt dirty just writing them. Unless you write kids' books, clichés are bad. Say it. Say it again, and then tattoo it on your sweaty forehead.

But there are things that have a sense of familiarity that do need to be included in your stories. These are called tropes, and tropes are different to clichés.

A cliché is a word, phrase, expression or scene that has been overused to the point it's as dull as watching paint dry...see what I did there? It's predictable and unoriginal.

Tropes are reoccurring themes, concepts and patterns usually found embedded within genres. Tropes help you identify what genre you're reading. What separates a trope from a cliché is that a trope can be done over and over again, as long as it's told in a novel way each time.

If you write genre fiction, make sure you study your genre's tropes so you can use them wisely. Tropes are tropes for a reason: they work. People like them. Don't be an idiot and avoid them all to be unique because you'll write yourself out of your genre.

But likewise, you don't need to use *all* the tropes. Think of tropes as diamonds; every girl wants a diamond, but no one's rich enough to buy an entire ball gown made of ten carat diamonds, and if you are, bugger off and stop ruining my analogy.

QUICK TIP – History vs. Clichés. Some clichés are based on historical fact. For example, a cigar smoking gangster in a book set in the forties is totally valid, even though we might see it as somewhat clichéd. But in this instance, you can't avoid the cliché because you still need to create historical authenticity. So, the occasional cliché, especially when it represents a factual piece of history, is fine.

If you're freaking out because you have a ton of clichés in your story, fear not, dear wordsmither. You don't have to remove every single cliché. If you've used them in moderation, they fit a historical context, or they are subtle enough your beta readers skim over them, leave them be. But do read your genre. A lot. Dissect patterns, learn the tropes and make sure your villains have motives and reasons why they do things to prevent the cliché in the first place.

Classic Trope Examples:

Young Adult Tropes

- Orphan protagonist or distant parents
- Love triangles
- A graduation ceremony

Fantasy

- The chosen one
- The one magical sword/potion/device that will save the world and is conveniently difficult to locate
- Prophecy

Crime

- A dead body discovered at the start of a novel
- A crime fighting detective overly dedicated to the job
- A maverick detective
- A murderer either arrested or killed at the end of the book
- Serial killers

Romance Tropes

- Boy meets girl
- Enemies to lovers
- Forbidden lovers
- Matchmaker
- Societal class divide between love interests
- Happy ever after endings

Villainous Clichés

There are a ton of villainous clichés, and I won't list them all, but below is a short list, to give you a little flavor of what villain clichés look like:

- Black cats, parrots or pets of any variety attached to a

villain - think pirates with parrots or Dr. Evil's bald cat in
Austin Powers
- Phrases like, "I'm going to destroy the world" or "I'm going to rule the world"
- Dark hair, dark eyes, dark outfits. Anything associated with the color black
- Slick hair
- Disfigurements or scars
- Swagger
- Excessive arrogance
- Excessively charming
- Mental health disorders
- Lairs/dungeons/penthouses
- Delusions of grandeur
- Witches with black hats, pointy noses and a wart
- Witches with cackles or villains that go 'muhahaha'
- Excessive hyperbolic monologues
- Manners or posh accents (particularly British or Eastern European)
- A classical music lover
- A love of red wine / Chianti
- Fireplaces with roaring fires and logs
- Massive self-portraits hanging in lounges, lairs or offices
- Thrones or wing backed chairs
- Henchmen (although this one can also be a trope)
- If not henchmen, then minions or some kind of second in command that does all their bidding
- Evil with no motive
- Befriends the hero
- A villain that reveals his plan before acting on it
- Smoking
- Shaved heads
- Formerly imprisoned
- Loves their mother excessively
- Runs a secret society

- Bad childhood
- Voices in their head
- Extremist viewpoints

Villain Trope Examples

General Tropes

- Henchmen (genre dependent)
- Power hungry
- Wants to win at all costs
- Killing someone innocent

Dystopian

- A dinner feast/party/ball or major celebration hosted by the villain and representing the class difference
- A villain with a hard to argue with reasoning for the dystopian societal system

Thriller

- Helicopter or speed boat but some swanky method of escape
- Psychopath/sociopath
- Scantily clad women, serving a villain's every desire

Fantasy

- Wolves, dragons and snakes
- Dark magic

If you'd like more information on avoiding clichés then check out step 8 pages 116 to 127 in 13 Steps To Evil.

DEVELOPING MARKET KNOWLEDGE EXERCISES

Q. Name five villains you think are clichéd. Try to pick three from your genre.

A.1.

.

A.2.

.

A.3.

.

A.4.

.

A.5.

.

Q. Name five villain tropes from your genre.

A.1.

.

A.2.

.

A.3.

.

A.4.

.

A.5.

.

Q. Name five non-villain tropes from your genre.

A.1.

.

A.2.

.

A.3.

.

A.4.

.

A.5.

.

Q. Other than cigar smoking gangsters, can you think of three other examples of modern clichés derived from historical fact?

A.1.

.

A.2.

.

A.3.

.

DEVELOPING YOUR VILLAIN EXERCISES

Q. List ten other villainous clichés.

A.1.

.

A.2.

.

A.3.

.

A.4.

.

A.5.

.

A.6.

.

A.7.

.

A.8.

.

A.9.

.

A.10.

.

Q. Thinking about characters in general, what's your biggest pet hate, cliché or issue with characterization?

A.
.

.

.

.

•

Q. What, if any, clichés from the list above did you find in your work? And are they valid or if not, how will you change the plot to remove them?

A.

•

•

•

•

•

Q. What villain tropes are there in your genre? Name three.

A.1.

•

A.2.

•

A.3.

•

Q. Note down how you could weave one or two of them into your story.

A.

-

-

-

-

-

STEP 9 FEAR AND PHOBIAS

There's a difference between horror and your villain. Villain's don't need to come from the horror genre to be villainous. They just have to use the idea of fear to scare a reader. Why? Because readers don't need real monsters to scare them, monsters are already in their head.

Psychologists will tell you that thinking or imagining an activity, like say, playing tennis, will light up the same areas of the brain as when you actually play tennis, albeit to a lesser extent. So the same method can be applied to fear.

And just what is fear?

Fear is an emotion caused by a perceived threat of pain or harm; fear is irrational.

Publishing, like the film industry, cycles between different types of horror and fear. Psychological and physiological are the two most relevant to novel writers.

QUICK TIP – Physiological Fear is created by what you can see such as blood, gore, and the threat of pain.

QUICK TIP - Psychological Fear is created not by what you can see, like gore or a weapon, but by what you can't.

We can learn a lot from films by using their tactics of implication and insinuation to induce fear. Think about the last film you watched. When the tension rises, the music changes, a quick flash to a missing knife, a few drops of blood, and a door left open.

The point is, a reader's imagination is stronger and more powerful than our words will ever be. Work with it and use their imagination to your advantage.

How? Use all five senses in your writing. Withholding information purposefully, misdirecting, and a hint at evil is enough to get readers twitchy because if your protagonist is scared your reader will be too.

QUICK TIP – Context Matters. What creates the sphincter tightening scare factor is not the gore but the context surrounding it. It's not the fact a knife is missing or a door has been left open, it's the knowledge that that particular door hasn't been opened in a decade.

If you'd like more information on creating fear then check step 9 pages 128 to 138 in 13 Steps To Evil.

DEVELOPING MARKET KNOWLEDGE EXERCISES

Q. Name five villains from a mix of books and films that have scared you a little bit.

A.1.

.

A.2.

.

A.3.

.

A.4.

.

A.5.

.

Q. Name three films or books that use gore to create fear.

A.1.

.

A.2.

.

A.3.

.

Q. Name three films or books that use psychological techniques to create fear.

A.1.

.

A.2.

.

A.3.

.

Q. What tactics do they use that you can replicate in your story?

A.

.

.

.

.

.

Q. What type of fear do you find most in your genre?

A.

.

.

.

.

.

DEVELOPING YOUR VILLAIN EXERCISES

Q. Do you use fear in your story? If so, are you using psychological or physiological fear? Or both?

A.

.

.

.

.

.

Q. Everyone is afraid of something. What are you afraid of?

A.

.

.

.

.

.

Q. How could you use that fear in your novel to increase tension and conflict?

A.

.

.

.

.

.

Q. Can you name any other fears? Write a list as long as you can of fears characters could have that would fit your story.

A.1.

.

A.2.

.

A.3.

.

A.4.

.

A.5.

.

A.6.

.

A.7.

.

A.8.

.

A.9.

.

A.10.

.

Q. Watch the news every day for a week. What are the five worst stories you heard? How could you incorporate those into your characters?

A.1.

.

A.2.

.

A.3.

.

A.4.

•

A.5.

•

Q. What is your hero afraid of?

A.

•

•

•

•

Q. How will your villain use this fear to put a barrier in the way of your hero?

A.

•

•

•

•

Q. What change or personal growth does your hero need to go through to defeat his fear and beat your villain?

A.

.

.

.

.

Q. What is your villain afraid of?

A.

.

.

.

.

Q. How will your hero use this fear to defeat your villain?

A.

.

.

.

.

EXERCISE: Write a paragraph where your villain scares your hero.

A.

．

．

．

．

EXERCISE: Now write a paragraph where something scares your villain.

A.

．

．

．

．

EXERCISE: Write a paragraph using all five senses to create fear.

A.

．

．

．

．

．

.

.

.

Q. Note down three tactics your villain uses from movie making tactics like insinuation to 'show' rather than 'tell' how significant their threats are.

A.1.

.

A.2.

.

A.3.

.

Q. What information do you purposely withhold from your hero?

A.

.

.

.

.

STEP 10 MENTAL HEALTH

One of the biggest challenges with writing villains is that stories are usually told from the point of view of the hero. You have to write concisely to create a convincing villain. But in doing this, writers sometimes take shortcuts to make their bad guy as villainous as possible. One of those shortcuts is giving your villain a mental health disorder. There are two problems with that:

1. The disorders aren't always portrayed accurately.
2. It leads to myths, misconceptions and stigmatizing a sector of society.

Let me be clear; I am **not** suggesting people or characters with mental health issues are all villains or antagonists. What I'm saying is that **some** of the great villains in literary and film history have these disorders. **What's unfortunate is that they can be portrayed in a clichéd or subtly discriminatory way.**

Now because this is a workbook and there are far too many important aspects of each disorder, I won't summarize. There is more detailed information in the full textbook version of 13 Steps To Evil. If you'd like more information on the common disorders, check step 10 in 13 Steps To Evil pages 139 to 158.

The common disorders are:

- Schizophrenia
- Multiple Personality Disorder
- Borderline Personality Disorder (often used with female villains)
- Obsessive Compulsive Disorder (OCD)
- Antisocial Personality Disorder (also known as Psychopathy and Sociopathy)
- Narcissistic Personality Disorder
- Bipolar Disorder (becoming more common)

If you choose to use a mental health disorder in one of your characters, make sure you do your research.

QUICK TIP: Research this if your villain has a mental health disorder.

- The illness in its entirety
- Medication (and side effects)
- Symptomology
- Patterns of behavior
- Triggers
- Severity
- Coping strategies
- Reactions to stress or emotional situations
- Prevalence
- Comorbidities
- Whether or not a person is aware of their disorder and treatments

In reality when a person has a mental health disorder, the chances are they have more than one. Having a mental health disorder often (although not always) changes the brain's chemistry. This means that the brain is more susceptible to having a second, third or even fourth mental health disorder. This is called **comorbidity.**

For example, people with schizophrenia can suffer from additional mental health disorders like:

- *Substance abuse*
- *Anxiety, and depression*
- *OCD (obsessive compulsive disorder)*
- *PTSD (post-traumatic stress disorder)*
- *Panic disorder*

QUICK TIP - Don't be afraid to give your villain more than one disorder.

You don't have to be explicit or use obvious exposition in the narrative to tell the reader what disorders they have, you can allude to their symptoms through their behavior, body language, and dialogue.

DEVELOPING MARKET KNOWLEDGE EXERCISES

Q. Can you list three villains from your genre (or another if you can't get three from yours) with each disorder?

Schizophrenia

A.1.

.

A.2.

.

A.3.

.

Multiple Personality Disorder

A.1.

.

A.2.

.

A.3.

.

Borderline Personality Disorder

A.1.

.

A.2.

.

A.3.

.

Obsessive Compulsive Disorder

A.1.

.

A.2.

.

A.3.

.

Antisocial Personality Disorder

A.1.

.

A.2.

.

A.3.

.

Narcissistic Personality Disorder

A.1.

.

A.2.

.

A.3.

.

Bipolar Disorder

A.1.

.

A.2.

.

A.3.

.

Q. List five heroes with disorders from your genre.

A.1.

.

A.2.

.

A.3.

.

A.4.

.

A.5.

.

DEVELOPING YOUR VILLAIN EXERCISES

If your villain has a mental health disorder fill out the answers to the research questions below:

Q. What is the disorder?

A.

.

.

.

Q. What medication would a sufferer use? And are there side effects?

A.

.

.

.

.

.

.

Q. What is the common symptomology?

A.

-

-

-

-

-

-

Q. What are the common patterns of behavior, coping strategies, and reactions under stressful or emotional situations?

A.

-

-

-

-

-

-

Q. Are there any triggers?

A.

·

·

·

·

·

·

Q. What are the common patterns of behavior?

A.

·

·

·

·

·

·

Q. What is the prevalence of the disorder? And what comorbid disorders might they suffer from?

A.

·

.

.

.

.

.

Q. Will your villain be aware of their disorder?

A.

.

.

.

.

.

.

Q. If your villain has a comorbid disorder, what affect will this have on their behavior?

A.

.

.

.

.

.

.

If they do have a comorbid disorder, then use the questions below to aid your research.

Q. What is the disorder?

A.

.

.

.

Q. What medication would a sufferer use? And are there side effects?

A.

.

.

.

.

.

.

Q. What is the common symptomology?

A.

.

.

.

.

.

.

Q. What are the common patterns of behavior, coping strategies, and reactions under stressful or emotional situations?

A.

.

.

.

.

.

.

Q. Are there any triggers?

A.

·

·

·

·

·

·

Q. What are the common patterns of behavior?

A.

·

·

·

·

·

·

Q. What is the prevalence of the disorder? And what comorbid disorders might they suffer from?

A.

.

.

.

.

.

.

Q. Will your villain be aware of their disorder?

A.

.

.

.

.

.

.

Q. Does your villain need any events woven into their past to have caused their illness? If yes, what are they?

A.

-
-
-
-
-
-

STEP 11 CONFLICT AND CLIMAX

Conflict

Conflict is the foundation of every novel. Without it, your book flat lines like the Grim Reaper. No self-respecting book doctor will attempt to resuscitate it. Even a shot of conflict-adrenaline might not save it because conflict is story-oxygen, and without bags of it, your book will stay six-feet under.

Conflict can come from anywhere and any character in your novel. **But the main source should always be your antagonist or villain.**

QUICK TIP – Specificity Rules. Your conflict needs to be specific. Don't have a war with a million minions if you can't identify why it's happening. It's also useful to link the conflict to your hero's and villain's goals.
You need to link the conflict to their goals because it makes your characters emotionally invested in the battle, and if your characters are, then your readers will be too.

QUICK TIP - Tick Tock. Time pressure makes conflict more intense.

It raises the stakes and takes away a bit more of your hero's hope that he can win in time.

Raise the stakes even further by making whatever the villain wants important to the hero.

Climax

Your climax is the pinnacle of your story and no matter what the theatrics and dramatic surroundings are, it's only ever about two people: hero and villain.

Why? Because that's what stories are: the interaction, relationship, impact and effect one person has on another.

No matter who's fighting in the final showdown, the only action that matters to your reader is what occurs between your hero and your villain. Make sure the focus is on them, what they do, and what happens to them.

This is why whatever action annihilates the villain, must come from the hero, and likewise, the conflict leading up to your climax must be driven by the villain.

QUICK TIP – Hero's Arc. For your hero to win, he has to change. Part of his character arc must lead him to change as a person, see the world differently, or realise his mistakes. It's only once he's had these revelations that he can become the person he needs to be to beat your villain.

Sometimes there's a great villain speech or monologue near the climax of a story. If you use one, then their speech needs to do two things to pack the power of a literary Oscar.

1. State the villain's intention
2. Convince the reader the villain is right, even if just for a second

If you'd like more information on creating climaxes and conflict then check step 11 pages 158 to 174 in 13 Steps To Evil.

DEVELOPING MARKET KNOWLEDGE EXERCISES

Q. Think about the last five books or films you read/watched in your genre. Identify the main conflict between the hero and villain.

A.1.

.

A.2.

.

A.3.

.

A.4.

.

A.5.

.

Q. Are there any patterns to the conflict?

A.

.

.

-

-

-

-

Q. In the five stories you just mentioned what types of battles or fights happen during the climax?

A.1.

-

A.2.

-

A.3.

-

A.4.

-

A.5.

-

Q. What is it about each story's conflict that makes it specific?

A.1.

.

A.2.

.

A.3.

.

A.4.

.

A.5.

.

Q. How is the conflict linked to the hero's and villain's goals or motives?

A.1.

.

A.2.

.

A.3.

.

A.4.

.

A.5.

.

Q. Note down the change each hero went through to beat the villain.

A.1.

.

A.2.

.

A.3.

.

A.4.

.

A.5.

.

Q. Pick your favorite story from the five above. Deconstruct the plot and note down every new layer of tension or conflict. What does this show you about story construction, and what reflections can you make on your own plot?

A.

.

.

.

.

DEVELOPING YOUR VILLAIN EXERCISES

Q. What is the primary conflict in your novel?

A.

.

.

.

.

Q. How is it linked to your hero's and villain's goals or motives?

A.

.

.

.

.

Q. Write down three ways you could add time pressure to either the story you're working on or the last book you read.

A.1.

.

A.2.

.

A.3.

.

Q. How do you raise the stakes in your story?

A.

.

.

.

.

.

Q. What change will your hero go through to beat your villain?

A.

.

.

.

.

Q. Does your climax focus on the hero and villain? If not, what do you need to change to ensure it does?

A.

.

.

.

.

Q. Look at your plot. Can you identify the moment your hero moves from reactive to proactive? Can you identify the scene or action your villain takes around the middle of your book that forces the hero's change?

A.

.

.

.

.

.

STEP 12 ONCE UPON A TIME… HAPPILY NEVER AFTER

There are various types of ending but like the types of villain archetype, they too can be archetyped.

Happily Ever After:

QUICK TIP – HEA. Happily Ever After is often referred to as HEA.

Your villain's stuffed. He has to die. But the most important part of an HEA is that the villain dies *at the hand of your hero.* Usually found in kids' books, fairy tales and romance.

Not So Happily Ever After:

The important thing is the hero most definitely, does not win. Or if he does, he suffers such significant losses in the process, it isn't worth it. There's a lot of loss and death during the story. The villain, while he may not win in the purest sense (because how often does the villain ever win?), something really chuffing bad happens to whatever characters do survive.

Above all, you need to foreshadow this ending earlier on in your story because it's unusual so your readers won't expect it. If you don't foreshadow the impending loss, your readers will feel cheated. That doesn't mean you need to give your plot's climax away, just do a Hansel and Gretel and leave bookish breadcrumbs in your chapters.

Hero's Sacrifice:

Your villain should have put obstacles in your hero's way to result in her needing to sacrifice something to win.

QUICK TIP – Sacrifice And Themes. More often than not the hero's sacrifice becomes a theme or subplot rather than the actual book ending. Most writers shy away from using a hero's sacrifice because it closes off their story to any sequels (and that loses money).

Your biggest problem as a writer with this type of ending is finding a solution to who narrates the ending.

Bittersweet:

Bittersweet endings mix pleasure with pain. The hero needs to lose something significant, something that means the world to them. Whatever they lose needs to be significant enough it changes them forever.

A bittersweet ending needs two things to happen to a hero: something positive and something negative.

Ambiguous Endings:

Ambiguous ending are mainly found in literary fiction but sometimes in other genres too. These endings have a subplot or storyline left open enough that one of two possible outcomes could have happened and it's for the reader to interpret and decide which ending happened.

If you leave an ending open, you need to make sure that every other subplot and storyline is 100% closed off with no possibility of alternative outcomes, or your story will feel unfinished.

If you'd like more information on endings then check step 12 pages 175 to 191 in 13 Steps To Evil.

DEVELOPING MARKET KNOWLEDGE EXERCISES

Q. Name three stories in your genre with an HEA.

A.1.

•

A.2.

•

A.3.

•

Q. Name three stories in your genre with a not so HEA.

A.1.

•

A.2.

•

A.3.

•

Q. Name three stories in your genre with a hero's sacrifice.

A.1.

.

A.2.

.

A.3.

.

Q. Name three stories in your genre with a bittersweet ending.

A.1.

.

A.2.

.

A.3.

.

Q. If you can, name three stories in your genre with an ambiguous ending.

A.1.

.

A.2.

.

A.3.

.

Q. Think about the last five books or films you read/watched in your genre. Note down the ending they have.

A.1.

.

A.2.

.

A.3.

.

A.4.

.

A.5.

.

Q. Which type of ending was the easiest to identify? Is one type of ending more commonly found in your genre?

A.

•

•

•

•

Q. Think about your favorite villain. What is their ending? Do you like that particular villain because of the ending, or in spite of it?

A.

•

•

•

•

DEVELOPING YOUR VILLAIN EXERCISES

Q. What type of ending does your story have?

- Happily ever after
- Not so happily ever after
- Hero's sacrifice
- Bittersweet
- Ambiguous

Q. Thinking about all of the book endings you've noted above, which endings do you (as a reader) find most satisfying? Ask yourself why that is. Now do the same but as a writer, what is the most enjoyable ending to write?

Reader

Writer

Q. If you're writing a series, how many different types of endings will you need to use? Note them all down in series order.

A.

.

.

.

.

Q. How does your villain make your hero suffer for his win?

A.

.

.

.

.

Q. What does your hero have to sacrifice to beat your villain?

A.

.

.

.

.

Q. What's the best ending you've ever read? And why?

A.

.

.

.

.

STEP 13 INTRODUCING THE VILLAIN

Introducing the villain, like a lot of the concepts in this book, is genre dependent.

A lot of stories don't want the reader to know who the villain is right away. But diverting attention away from the villain isn't as easy as making the protagonist think someone else is the bad guy. If your protagonist places too much emphasis on another character as the villain, it becomes obvious to the reader that he isn't your man.

QUICK TIP – Everyone's A Bad Guy. Instead of placing the blame on another character, have several that create doubt and raise questions.

Assume your readers know everything, because, they do. Don't repeat information but give clues in the subtlest way possible because our readers are smart arses that pick up on everything.

QUICK TIP – The Righteous Villain. Try to avoid making your villain righteous or 'good' as a tactic to cast doubt in the reader's mind. Making them appear the exact opposite of what they are is a cliché, and your reader will see through it. Likewise, don't make them too evil, because that's obvious too. Like your mummy always said, everything in moderation, dear. Including your villain's extremes.

Even if you don't want your villain to be revealed until the end of your book, you need to introduce either them or the concept of them early on to prevent your reader feeling cheated. Feed clues into their unconscious mind so that when they do work out who the bad guy is, it's both plausible and believable.

The reason you need to introduce the concept of your villain early on is **because your reader needs to know what is at stake for your hero**, and the thing that creates the stakes for your hero is the villain.

If you'd like more information on introducing your villain then check step 13 pages 192 to 198 in 13 Steps To Evil.

DEVELOPING MARKET KNOWLEDGE EXERCISES

Q. Think about your five favorite villains. For each one, note down how they are they introduced and at what point in the plot.

Villain 1

.

.

.

.

Villain 2

.

.

.

.

Villain 3

.

.

.

.

Villain 4

.

.

.

.

Villain 5

.

.

.

.

Q. Do you find out what the villain's goal is during his introduction? If yes, note it down.

A.1.

.

A.2.

.

A.3.

.

A.4.

.

A.5.

.

Q. Are there any patterns or tropes as to how a villain is introduced in your genre?

A.

.

.

.

.

.

Q. Which characters in the above stories were suspicious enough to cast doubt over the real villain's identity?

A.

.

-

-

-

-

DEVELOPING YOUR VILLAIN EXERCISES

Q. At what point in your plot is your villain introduced?

A.

-

-

-

-

-

Q. If late on in the plot, what clues will you give the reader, and when?

A.

-

-

-

-

·

Q. Which characters in your book are dubious enough to cast doubt over who the real villain is?

A.

·

·

·

·

·

Q. If you don't introduce your villain early on, how do you show the reader what's at stake for your hero?

A.

·

·

·

·

·

THANK YOU

Thank you for reading the 13 Steps To Evil Workbook. I hope you found it helpful as you created your villain.

If you loved the book and can spare a few minutes, I would be really grateful for a short review on the site you purchased the book. Your support is appreciated.

If you would like to hear more about future publications or receive the checklist I mentioned, please sign up **here**.

http://eepurl.com/bRLqwT

ABOUT THE AUTHOR

Sacha Black is an author, rebel podcaster, speaker and developmental editor. She has five obsessions; words, expensive shoes, conspiracy theories, self-improvement, and breaking the rules. She also has the mind of a perpetual sixteen-year-old, only with slightly less drama and slightly more bills.

Sacha writes books about people with magical powers and other books about the art of writing. She lives in Hertfordshire, England, with her wife and genius, giant of a son.

When she's not writing, she can be found laughing inappropriately loud, blogging, sniffing musty old books, fangirling film and TV soundtracks, or thinking up new ways to break the rules.

http://eepurl.com/bRLqwT

www.sachablack.co.uk
sachablack@sachablack.co.uk

instagram.com/sachablackauthor
bookbub.com/authors/sacha-black
facebook.com/sachablackauthor
twitter.com/sacha_black
amazon.com/author/sachablack

ALSO BY SACHA BLACK

10 Steps to Hero - How to Craft a Kickass Protagonist (and Workbook) For Writers

From cardboard cut-out to superhero in 10 steps.

Are you fed up of one-dimensional heroes? Frustrated with creating clones? Does your protagonist fail to capture your reader's heart?

In 10 Steps To Hero, you'll discover:

+ How to develop a killer character arc

+ A step-by-step guide to creating your hero from initial concept to final page

+ Why the web of story connectivity is essential to crafting a hero that will hook readers

+ The four major pitfalls to avoid as well as the tropes your story needs

Finally, there is a comprehensive writing guide to help you create your perfect protagonist. Whether you're writing your first story or you're a professional writer, this book will help supercharge your hero and give them that extra edge.

These lessons will help you master your charming knights, navigate your way to the perfect balance of flaws and traits, as well as strengthen your hero to give your story the conflict and punch it needs.

First, there were villains, now there are heroes. If you like dark humor, learning through examples, and want to create the best hero you can, then you'll love Sacha Black's guide to crafting heroes.

Read 10 Steps To Hero today and start creating kick-ass heroes.

10 Steps To Hero: How To Craft A Kickass Protagonist

10 Steps To Hero - How To Craft A Kickass Protagonist Workbook

ALSO BY SACHA BLACK

The Anatomy of Prose: 12 Steps to Sensational Sentences

Do your sentences fail to sound the way you want? Are they lackluster, with flat characters and settings? Is your prose full of bad habits and crutches?

In The Anatomy of Prose, you'll discover:

- A step-by-step guide to creating descriptions that sing
- The key to crafting character emotions that will hook a reader
- How to harness all five senses to make your stories come alive, deepening your reader's experience
- Tips and tricks for balancing details at the sentence level
- Methods for strengthening each sentence through strategic word choice, rhythm and flow
- Dozens of literary devices, and how to utilize them to give your prose power
- Tactics for differentiating characters in dialogue as well as making it punchy and unforgettable
- A comprehensive prose-specific self-editing check list
- How to embody your character's personality at the sentence level

- The most common pitfalls and mistakes to avoid

The Anatomy of Prose is a comprehensive writing guide that will help you create sensational sentences. Whether you're just starting out or are a seasoned writer, this book will power up your prose, eliminate line-level distractions and help you find the perfect balance of show and tell. By the end of this book, you'll know how to strengthen your sentences to give your story, prose and characters the extra sparkle they need to capture a reader's heart.

If you like dark humor, learning through examples and want to create perfect prose, then you'll love Sacha Black's guide to crafting sensational sentences. Read **The Anatomy of Prose** today and start creating kick-ass stories.

The Anatomy of Prose: 12 Steps to Sensational Sentences

The Anatomy of Prose: 12 Steps to Sensational Sentences Workbook

ACKNOWLEDGMENTS

Writers often see themselves as lone wolves, tapping away at the keyboard night after night. But it's not true. Not really. Every writer has a pack of wolves: friends, family, children, writing buddies, editors, designers and supporters, who group together and help an author to the finish line. Without them, this book would never have happened.

To my wife first, thank you for being so patient, for letting me follow my dream, and for putting up with the incessant tapping in the back of the living room. My son, for inspiring me to be a role model, and giving me the drive to show him you have to follow your dreams no matter what. Mum and Dad, thanks for, you know, doing it, and making an awesome kid.

My accountability partner, Allie Potts, for dragging my ass kicking and screaming to the finish line.

The Bloggers Bash committee, Ali, Geoff and Hugh, for the unending support and reassurance. I've no idea how you put up with me.

Suzie and Lucy, for listening to me on a daily basis and coaxing me off the cliff edge when my self-doubt reared its ugly head... Repeatedly.

To my blogging friends, too many to mention, thank you for the continuous support, listening to my rambles, grumbles and excessive swearing!

To Dr. Amy Murphy, for years of friendship and for being the shrink I never could, thank you for correcting my rusty brain.

To the hundreds of writers, bloggers, friends and readers who filled out my research survey and made this book possible, I am indebted.

Last, and most importantly, thank you to you, the readers, for taking the time to buy and read this book. I hope it's been helpful, and I wish you success in your writing career.

FURTHER READING

The Writer's Guide to Character Traits, by Dr. Linda N. Edelstein:

The Emotion Thesaurus by Angela Ackerman and Becca Puglisi:

The Negative Trait Thesaurus by Angela Ackerman and Becca Puglisi:

The Positive Trait Thesaurus by Angela Ackerman and Becca Puglisi:

The Psychology of Superheroes – An Unauthorized Exploration, Edited by Robin S. Rosenberg, PhD

The Writer's Guide To Psychology by Carolyn Kaufman

VILLAIN INTERVIEW

Q. Describe your villain's general appearance e.g. age, height, name, eye color, hair color, voice, stature, distinguishing features like birth-marks, scars or tattoos and general attire.

A.

.

.

.

Q. Are there any interesting stories behind the distinguishing features?

A.

.

.

.

Q. What are your villain's negative traits?

Trait 1

-

-

-

Trait 2

-

-

-

Trait 3

-

-

-

Q. What are your villain's positive traits?

Trait 1

-

-

-

Trait 2

-

-

-

Trait 3

-

-

-

Q. Who are the character's friends/family/key relationships?

A.

-

-

-

Q. What or who would they die for?

A.

-

-

-

Q. What does love feel like to them?

A.

-

-

-

Q. Have they ever been in love?

A.

.

.

.

Q. Are they capable of loving someone or something?

A.

.

.

.

Q. What does success look like to them?

A.

.

.

.

Q. What are their positive soul scars?

A.

.

.

.

Q. What are their negative soul scars?

A.

.

.

.

Q. What's their worst memory?

A.

.

.

.

Q. What's their happiest memory?

A.

.

.

.

Q. Are they afraid of anything?

A.

.

.

.

Q. What's their deepest desire?

A.

.

.

.

Q. What are their negative traits?

A.

.

.

.

Q. What are their positive traits?

A.

.

.

.

Q. What's their greatest achievement?

A.

.

.

.

Q. Have they ever sacrificed their desires for someone else?

A.

.

.

.

Q. What are the most significant events in their lives?

A.

.

.

.

Q. Are they proud of anything?

A.

.

.

.

Q. Are they ashamed of anything?

A.

.

.

.

Q. What's the worst thing they've ever done?

A.

.

.

.

Q. What's their relationship like with their parents?

A.

.

.

.

Q. What was their childhood like?

A.

.

.

.

Q. Do they have any misperceptions about the world?

A.

.

.

.

Q. What lie do they believe?

A.

.

.

.

Q. Who would they call in the middle of the night when they are in trouble?

A.

.

.

.

Q. How do they generally interact with people? Cold? Friendly? Warm?

A.

.

.

.

Q. What's their relationship with their parents like?

A.

.

.

.

Q. What is their goal/motivation/priority within the plot?

A.

.

.

.

Q. What would they do to get it? And why?

A.

.

.

.

Q. Who would they die for?

A.

.

.

.

Q. Who would they kill for?

A.

.

.

.

Q. Who or what could make them lie?

A.

.

.

.

Q. What could make them cry?

A.

.

.

.

Q. What makes them laugh/smile?

A.

.

.

.

Q. What's their greatest regret?

A.

.

.

.

Q. What's their greatest achievement?

A.

.

.

.

Q. What's their biggest failure?

A.

.

.

.

Q. What's their happiest memory?

A.

.

.

.

Q. What talents do they have?

A.

.

.

.

NON-EXHAUSTIVE LIST OF FICTIONAL
BOOK AND MOVIE VILLAINS

1. Dracula from *Dracula*
2. Vito Corleone from the *Godfather*
3. Freddy Krueger from *A Nightmare on Elm Street*
4. Jack Colby from *High Noon*
5. Ernst Stavro Blofeld from *You Only Live Twice*
6. Jud Casper from *Kes*
7. Lago from *Othello*
8. Darth Vader from *Star Wars*
9. Annie Wilkes from *Misery*
10. Red Grant from *Russia With Love*
11. Alex Forrest from *Fatal Attraction*
12. Travis Bickle from *Taxi Driver*
13. Colonel Walter E. Kurtz from *Apocalypse Now*
14. The Child Catcher from *Chitty Chitty Bang Bang*
15. The Joker from *The Dark Knight*
16. Bane from *The Dark Knight Rises*
17. Alex DeLarge from *A Clockwork Orange*
18. Lord Voldemort from *Harry Potter and The Philosopher's Stone*
19. The Monster from *Frankenstein*

20. Norman Bates from *Psycho*
21. The Wicked Witch of the West from *The Wizard of Oz*
22. Tommy DeVito from *Goodfellas*
23. Richard III from *Richard III*
24. Amon Goeth from *Schindler's List*
25. Nurse Ratched from *One Flew Over the Cuckoo's Nest*
26. Hannibal Lecter from *Silence of The Lambs*
27. Joan Crawford from *Mummy Dearest*
28. Gunnery Sgt Hartman from *Full Metal Jacket*
29. The Evil Queen from *Snow White and The Seven Dwarfs*
30. Cruella De Ville from *101 Dalmatians*
31. The Sheriff of Nottingham from *Robin Hood*
32. Leatherface from *Texas Chainsaw Massacre*
33. Keyser Soze from *The Usual Suspects*
34. Hans Gruber from *Die Hard*
35. Hans Landa from *Inglorious Bastards*
36. Jack Torrance from *The Shining*
37. Clarence Boddicker from *Robocop*
38. General Zod from *Superman II*
39. Michael Myers from *Halloween*
40. Anton Chigurh from *No Country for Old Men*
41. John Doe from *Seven*
42. Auric Goldfinger from *Goldfinger*
43. HAL 9000 from *2001 A Space Odyssey*
44. The Alien from *Alien*
45. T-1000 from *Terminator 2: Judgement Day*
46. Agent Smith from *The Matrix*
47. Gordon Gecko from *Wall Street*
48. Dudley Smith from *LA Confidential*
49. Frank Booth from *Blue Velvet*
50. Ivan Drago from *Rocky*
51. Begbie from *Trainspotting*
52. Russ Cargill from *The Simpsons Movie*
53. Davy Jones from *Pirates of the Caribbean*
54. Captain Barbossa from *Pirates of the Caribbean*

55. Count Olaf from the *Lemony Snicket - A Series of Unfortunate Events*
56. The Green Goblin from *Spider-Man*
57. President Snow from *The Hunger Games* by Suzanne Collins
58. Amy Dunne from *Gone Girl* by Gillian Flynn
59. Tom Ripley from *The Talented Mr. Ripley*
60. Moriarty from *The Final Problem* by Sir Arthur Conan Doyle
61. Steerpike from *Titus Groan and Gormenghast* by Mervyn Peake
62. Shere Khan from *The Jungle Book* by Rudyard Kipling
63. The White Witch from *The Lion, The Witch and The Wardrobe* by C.S. Lewis
64. Milo Minderbinder from *Catch 22* by Joseph Heller
65. Fred from the *Handmaid's Tale* by Margaret Atwood
66. Grendel's Mother from *Beowulf*
67. O'Brien from *Nineteen Eighty-Four* by George Orwell
68. Captain Hook from *Peter And Wendy* by J.M. Barrie
69. Ms Coulter from *His Dark Materials* trilogy by Philip Pullman
70. Clare Quilty from *Lolita* by Vladimir Nabokov
71. Bill Sykes from *Oliver Twist* by Charles Dickens
72. Sauron from *The Lord of the Rings* by J.R.R. Tolkien
73. Mr. Hyde from *The Strange Case of Dr. Jekyll and Mr. Hyde,* by Robert Louis Stevenson
74. Satan from *Paradise Lost* by John Milton

NON-EXHAUSTIVE LIST OF ANTI-HEROES

1. Beetlejuice from *Beetlejuice*
2. Deadpool
3. Suicide squad
4. Jordan Belfort from *The Wolf of Wall Street*
5. Jason Bourne from the *Jason Bourne* movies based on the books by Robert Ludlum
6. Chev Chelios from *Crank*
7. John Constantine from *Constantine*
8. Judge Dredd from *Dredd*
9. Hellboy from *Hellboy*
10. Jack Reacher from the *Jack Reacher* series
11. Shrek from *Shrek*
12. Captain Jack Sparrow from *Pirates of the Caribbean*
13. V from *V for Vendetta*
14. Theodore 'T-Bag' Bagwell from *Prison Break*
15. Jack Bauer from *24*
16. Edmund Blackadder from the BBC's *Blackadder* series
17. Chuck Bass from *Gossip Girl*
18. Nicholas Brody from *Homeland*
19. Saul Goodman from *Better Call Saul* and *Breaking Bad*

20. Jimmy McNulty from *The Wire*
21. Dexter Morgan from *Dexter*
22. Tony Soprano from *The Sopranos*
23. Walter White from *Breaking Bad*
24. Magneto and Wolverine from the *X-men*
25. Patrick Bateman from *American Psycho*
26. Miranda Priestly from *The Devil Wears Prada*

Negative Traits Listing			
Abrasive	Abrupt	Agonizing	Aggressive
Aimless	Airy	Aloof	Amoral
Angry	Anxious	Apathetic	Arbitrary
Argumentative	Arrogant	Artificial	Asocial
Assertive	Astigmatic	Authoritarian	Barbaric
Bewildered	Bizarre	Bland	Blunt
Boisterous	Brittle	Brutal	Business-like
Calculating	Callous	Cantankerous	Careless
Cautious	Charmless	Childish	Clumsy
Coarse	Cold	Colorless	Complacent
Complaintive	Compulsive	Conceited	Condemnatory
Confidential	Conformist	Conservative	Cowardly
Crafty	Crass	Crazy	Criminal
Critical	Crude	Cruel	Cynical
Decadent	Deceitful	Delicate	Demanding
Dependent	Desperate	Destructive	Devious
Difficult	Dirty	Disconcerting	Discontented
Discouraging	Dishonest	Disloyal	Disobedient
Disorderly	Disorganized	Disputatious	Disrespectful
Disruptive	Dissolute	Dissonant	Distractible
Disturbing	Dogmatic	Domineering	Dull
Easily Discouraged	Egocentric	Enervated	Envious
Erratic	Escapist	Excitable	Expedient
Extravagant	Extreme	Faithless	False
Fanatical	Fanciful	Fatalistic	Fawning
Fearful	Fickle	Fiery	Fixed
Flamboyant	Foolish	Forgetful	Fraudulent
Frightening	Frivolous	Gloomy	Graceless
Grand	Greedy	Grim	Gullible
Hateful	Haughty	Hedonistic	Hesitant
Hidebound	High-handed	Hostile	Ignorant
Imitative	Impatient	Imprudent	Impulsive
Inconsiderate	Incurious	Indecisive	Indulgent
Inert	Inhibited	Insecure	Insensitive
Insincere	Insulting	Intolerant	Irascible
Irrational	Irresponsible	Irritable	Lazy
Libidinous	Loquacious	Malicious	Mannered
Manner-less	Mawkish	Mealy-mouthed	Mechanical
Meddlesome	Melancholic	Meretricious	Messy
Miserable	Miserly	Misguided	Mistaken
Money-minded	Monstrous	Moody	Morbid
Muddle-headed	Naive	Narcissistic	Narrow

Negative Traits Listing

Narrow-minded	Natty	Negativistic	Neglectful
Neurotic	Nihilistic	Obnoxious	Obsessive
Obvious	Odd	Offhand	One-dimensional
One-sided	Opinionated	Opportunistic	Oppressed
outrageous	Over-imaginative	Paranoid	Passive
Pedantic	Perverse	Petty	phlegmatic
Plodding	Pompous	Possessive	Power-hungry
Predatory	Prejudiced	Presumptuous	Pretentious
Prim	Procrastinating	Profligate	Provocative
Pugnacious	Puritanical	Quirky	Reactionary
Reactive	Regimental	Regretful	Repentant
Repressed	Resentful	Ridiculous	Rigid
Ritualistic	Rowdy	Ruined	Sadistic
Sanctimonious	Scheming	Scornful	Secretive
Sedentary	Selfish	Self-indulgent	Shallow
Short-sighted	Shy	Silly	Single-minded
Sloppy	Slow	Sly	Small-thinking
Softheaded	Sordid	Steely	Stiff
Strong-willed	Stupid	Submissive	Superficial
Superstitious	Tactless	Tasteless	Tense
Thievish	Thoughtless	Timid	Transparent
Treacherous	Trendy	Troublesome	Unappreciative
Uncaring	Uncharitable	Unconvincing	Uncooperative
Uncreative	Uncritical	Unctuous	Undisciplined
Unfriendly	Ungrateful	Unhealthy	Unimaginative
Unimpressive	Unlovable	Unmotivated	Unpolished
Unprincipled	Unrealistic	Unreflective	Unreliable
Unrestrained	Non-self-critical	Unstable	Vacuous
Vague	Venal	Venomous	Vindictive
Vulnerable	Weak	Weak-willed	Well-meaning
Willful	Wishful	Zany	

Accessible	Active	Adaptable	Admirable
Adventurous	Agreeable	Alert	Allocentric
Amiable	Anticipative	Appreciative	Articulate
Aspiring	Athletic	Attractive	Balanced
Benevolent	Brilliant	Calm	Capable
Captivating	Caring	Challenging	Charismatic
Charming	Cheerful	Clean	Clear-headed
Clever	Colorful	Companion	Compassionate
Conciliatory	Confident	Conscientious	Considerate
Constant	Contemplative	Cooperative	Courageous
Courteous	Creative	Cultured	Curious
Daring	Debonair	Decent	Decisive
Dedicated	Deep	Dignified	Directed
Disciplined	Discreet	Dramatic	Dutiful
Dynamic	Earnest	Ebullient	Educated
Efficient	Elegant	Eloquent	Empathetic
Energetic	Enthusiastic	Exciting	Extraordinary
Fair	Faithful	Farsighted	Felicific
Firm	Flexible	Focused	Forceful
Forgiving	Forthright	Freethinking	Friendly
Fun-loving	Gallant	Generous	Gentle
Liberal	Genuine	Good-natured	Gracious
Hardworking	Healthy	Hearty	Helpful
Heroic	High-minded	Honest	Honorable
Humble	Humorous	Idealistic	Imaginative
Impressive	Incisive	Incorruptible	Independent
Individualistic	Innovative	Inoffensive	Insightful
Insouciant	Intelligent	Intuitive	Invulnerable
Kind	Knowledgeable	Leader	Leisurely
Logical	Lovable	Loyal	Lyrical
Magnanimous	Many-sided	Masculine (or feminine)	Mature
Methodical	Meticulous	Moderate	Modest
Multileveled	Neat	Non-authoritarian	Objective
Open	Optimistic	Orderly	Organized
Original	Painstaking	Passionate	Patient
Patriotic	Sane	Peaceful	Perceptive
Perfectionist	Personable	Persuasive	Planner
Playful	Polished	Popular	Practical
Precise	Principled	Profound	Protean
Protective	Providential	Prudent	Punctual
Purposeful	Rational	Realistic	Reflective

Positive Traits Listing			
Relaxed	Reliable	Resourceful	Respectful
Responsible	Reverential	Romantic	Rustic
Sage	Scholarly	Scrupulous	Secure
Selfless	Self-critical	Self-denying	Self-reliant
Self-sufficient	Sensitive	Sentimental	Seraphic
Serious	Sexy	Sharing	Shrewd
Simple	Skillful	Sober	Sociable
Solid	Sophisticated	Spontaneous	Sporting
Stable	Steadfast	Steady	Stoic
Strong	Studious	Suave	Subtle
Sweet	Sympathetic	Systematic	Tasteful
Teacher	Thorough	Tidy	Tolerant
Tractable	Trusting	Uncomplaining	understanding
undogmatic	Unfoolable	Upright	Urbane
Venturesome	Vivacious	Warm	Well-bred
Well-read	Well-rounded	Winning	Wise
Witty	Youthful		

Neutral Traits Listing			
Absentminded	Ambitious	Amusing	Artful
Ascetic	Authoritarian	Big-thinking	Boyish
Breezy	Business-like	Busy	Casual
Cerebral	Chummy	Circumspect	Competitive
Complex	Confidential	Contradictory	Crisp
Cute	Deceptive	Determined	Dominating
Dreamy	Droll	Dry	Earthy
Effeminate	Emotional	Enigmatic	Experimental
Familial	Folksy	Formal	Freewheeling
Frugal	Glamorous	Guileless	High-spirited
Hurried	Hypnotic	Iconoclastic	Idiosyncratic
Impassive	Impersonal	Impressionable	Intense
Invisible	Irreligious	Irreverent	Maternal
Mellow	Modern	Moralistic	Mystical
Neutral	Noncommittal	Non-competitive	Obedient
Old-fashioned	ordinary	outspoken	Paternalistic
Physical	Placid	Political	Predictable
Preoccupied	Private	Progressive	Proud
Pire	Questioning	Quiet	Religious
Reserved	Restrained	Retiring	Sarcastic
Self-conscious	Sensual	Skeptical	smooth
Soft	Solemn	Solitary	Stern
Stolid	Strict	Stubborn	Stylish
Subjective	Surprising	Soft	Stern
Stolid	Strict	Stubborn	Stylish
Subjective	Surprising	Tough	Unaggressive
Unambitious	Unceremonious	Unchanging	Undemanding
Unfathomable	Unhurried	Uninhibited	Unpatriotic
Unpredictable	Unreligious	Unsentimental	Whimsical

Positive Values			
Authenticity	Accountability	Achievement	Adventure
Attractiveness	Balance	Challenge	Clarity
Commitment	Communication	Compassion	Competitiveness
Competency	Confidence	Continuous learning or growth	Courage
Creativity	Curiosity	Dependability	Determination
Discipline	Efficiency	Enthusiasm	Ethics
Excellence	Fairness	Flexibility	Freedom
Friendship	Generosity	Happiness	Health
Honesty	Humor	Independence	Integrity
Justice	Kindness	Knowledge	Leadership
Love	Loyalty	Openness	Optimism
Pleasure	Persistence	Respect	Security
Self-respect	Spirituality	Stability	Strength
Success	Support	Trustworthiness	Vision
Wisdom			

Negative Values			
Anger / Rage	Anxiety	Bitterness	Condemnation
Criticizing others	Cynicism	Depression	Despair
Despondency	Discouraging	Disinterested	Failure
Fame	Fear	Frustration	Gloom
Greed	Guilt	Helplessness	Hostility
Humiliation	Jealousy	Judgmental	Illness
Inequality	Lethargy	Loneliness	Misery
Ostracism	Pessimism	Pleasure	Regret
Rejection	Resignation	Rigidity	Sadness
Self-doubt	Sorrow	Status	Suspicion
Withdrawal	Worry		

Soul Scars			
Saved someone's life	Survived a car crash	Lost a limb	Went to war
Failed to make it to a deathbed	Divorced	Abandoned by parents/ lover/ sibling	Rejected by loved ones
Unrequited love	Failed	Continuous failure	Failed exams
Had to care for a loved one long term	Neglected as a child	Terminal illness	Lied to
Being cheated on	Victim of crime	Surgery	Addiction
Raped	Miscarried	Death of a child	Toxic friendship
Fell out of or lost friends	Involved in a cult	Lost religious belief	Witnessed cruelty or crime and weren't able to help
Experienced a natural disaster	Tornado	Hurricane	Earthquake
Tsunami	Bullied	Abused by parents/spouse	Manipulated
Death of a loved one	Lied to about your parentage or familial line/heritage	Was adopted	Lon period of unemployment
Kidnapped	Crossed a moral line to survive	Broke the law for the right reason	Made redundant
Sacked	Period of mental illness	Depression	